ALSO IN THE BLASTA BOOKS SERIES

Blasta Books #1: Tacos

Blasta Books #2: Hot Fat

Blasta Books #3: The United Nations of Cookies

Blasta Books #4: Wok

Blasta Books #5: Soup

Blasta Books #6: Tapas

Blasta Books #7: Wasted

Blasta Books #8: Masarap

Blasta Books #9: Funky

Blasta Books #10: Whole Catch

Blasta Books #11: Agak-Agak

blastabooks.com

SOCAFRO

Text by Alistair 'JD' Jeje
Illustrated by Nicky Hooper

CONTENTS

Introduction 1
The Socafro larder 6
Obe ata (Nigerian red sauce) 8

MEAT

Brown stew chicken 10
Nigerian red stew 12
Nigerian suya (spicy beef skewers) 14
Stuffed peppers 16
JD's jerk chicken curry 18
Charmaine's chicken soup with dumplings 20
Socafro fried chicken 22
Creamy coconut chicken curry 23
Nigerian pepper soup 24

SEAFOOD

Bake & hake 26
Trini curried prawns with coconut rice 28
Socafro smoked mackerel 30

EFO, EGUSI, EGGS

Efo riro 32
Egusi 33
Yam & eggs 34
Indomie & eggs 35

INTRODUCTION

I know what you're thinking. How did a guy from Lagos with an Afro-Caribbean background wind up in Waterford?

My mum was a midwife from Trinidad. Back when she did her training, a lot of women in Trinidad became teachers or nurses, and if you were a nurse, you left the country to study abroad. So she trained as a nurse in the UK. My dad was a Nigerian businessman who had moved to the UK. They met in Bristol, which is where I was born.

My dad lived in the UK for over 25 years but there was a boom in Nigeria, so he moved over to start investing there. My mum, my two older brothers, my older sister and I all moved too. My three younger siblings were born in Nigeria.

I did all my schooling in Nigeria, from primary school right through to university. When I left uni, my dad encouraged me to move back to the UK. I went to Yorkshire. I got my first job working as a waiter and expeditor, but I also got a job in retail at the same time.

I loved working in the restaurant, but my retail career took off. I started working in sales part time for the company Schuh in Leeds, but I quickly moved up the ladder – and moved around the country too. I moved from Leeds to Manchester, Stockport and Sheffield before being sent to Belfast in 2008 as senior deputy to shake things up there.

But after I got to Northern Ireland, my dad became ill with cancer. I left my job at the company and went back to Nigeria to be with him until he passed. By the time I'd looked after his estate, the recession had started. The pound and the euro had an equal value, so working in the Republic of Ireland instead of the North meant I could make more money. It was a no-brainer.

I got a job with Foot Locker and managed a store in Tallaght, then left there in 2011 to manage a store in Waterford and have been here ever since. At this point, the only place I've lived in longer than Waterford is Nigeria. It took me a long time to realise it, but Waterford feels like home now.

FROM FOOT LOCKER TO FOOD TRUCK

My mate Phil was the first person to plant the seed for Socafro in my head back in 2014, when I was still a manager at Foot Locker. He was selling coffee and I would go to his place for the chats. Normally we'd talk about trainers, but sometimes we'd talk about food. He told me I would do really well if I set up cooking my mum's recipes. And he didn't only say it to me once. He said it to me year after year.

At the time, I just couldn't see myself going into food. I'd say, 'Nah, I'm a successful store manager. That's not for me.'

And yet, I had this nagging feeling that there was something else I should be doing, that there was something else that makes me tick.

I played around with a few different entrepreneurial things on the side while I was still working at Foot Locker, but none of them were right.

Fast forward to 2020. The store closed down during the covid pandemic and all the staff were made redundant. It was only when everything ground to a halt and I had time to sit down and really think about what comes naturally to me that it hit me.

That thing that makes me tick? It's cooking.

Our second daughter was born on the first day of the lockdown, but my mum and my mother-in-law had already come over to help with the new baby. Between them, my wife and my two-year-old daughter, there were four women in the house who needed feeding! So I started cooking for everyone around me. It felt natural, easy.

Looking back, I've always loved cooking. When my mum or older sister would cook, I would listen to what they were saying and watch what they were doing. When other kids were outside playing, I'd be helping in the kitchen. I love food, and if you were helping in the kitchen, you'd always get more of it!

Six years after Phil first said it to me, I was finally ready to hear it. That's when I started Socafro Kitchen.

GOING ALL IN ON THE DREAM

I was at work at Foot Locker one day and told a colleague that I was thinking of starting a food truck but that I wasn't sure if I should go ahead with it. 'If you want to do this, just go right now and buy all the equipment,' he said. 'That way you'll be committed.'

'You know what?' I said. 'You're right.' So I went to Musgraves on my lunch break that same day and bought €1,500 of equipment in one go. The next day, I went back on my lunch break again and bought more. I either needed to go all in on this dream or back out altogether … but then I'd never know if it might have worked out.

My friend Wayne Halloran had his own food truck business, Hungary Bites. I wasn't even thinking of starting my own business at that time, but I liked what he was doing. I watched him start his business from scratch and studied everything he did, from how he set up his tent and applied to trade at festivals to asking him where he got his equipment. He's my mate and my mentor.

The whole time I was learning from Wayne, I knew I needed a place where I could set up and sell from. I heard about the Phoenix Yard, a food yard in the centre of town started by Keith Daniels that kept popping up on my Facebook feed, so I went to suss it out one night as a customer. The next week, I went back with a business proposal.

As soon as I told Keith that I wanted to do Afro-Caribbean fusion food, he pointed to an empty spot in the yard and said I could be set up and selling in four weeks. I thought it might take me four months! But six weeks to the day that I had that chat with Keith, I had set up Socafro Kitchen and started trading.

The first day, Keith was promoting me on Facebook and people were coming in. It was a sunny day and there was a good buzz. This couple came – the woman was American and I think the guy was from Croatia. They bought some food and sat down. A little while later, she came back and asked if she could speak to me in private.

She said, 'I just wanted to tell you that when my husband was trying your food, I could see him tearing up.' My heart started racing, thinking there was something wrong with the food. Had I put in too much pepper? 'This food reminds him so much of his late dad,' she continued. 'This is the type of food that he cooked.'

To this day, I still get emotional when I think about that. From that moment, I knew that this is what I should be doing. If I can get that kind of response on my very first day – if I can make someone feel that way – then this is it. This is my calling.

BLASTA BOOKS #12

THE SOCAFRO LARDER

The recipes in this book mostly use ingredients that you can get in any shop – I use lots of onions, tomatoes, peppers, chicken, beef and basmati rice – but cooked in ways you might never have tasted before. That's the fun of cooking!

There are some ingredients, though, that you'll need to make a special trip to an African shop for or source online.

1 Bean flour

2 Black-eyed beans

3 Crayfish seasoning

4 Egusi (ground melon seeds)

5 Gungo peas (aka pigeon peas)

6 Maggi stock cubes

7 Nigerian pepper soup mix

8 Palm oil

9 Scotch bonnet peppers

10 Suya spice mix

11 Yam and yam flour

HOW TO MAKE
ONE SAUCE, MANY DISHES

This tomato-pepper blend is the foundation of so many dishes – it's like the mother sauce of Nigerian cuisine. Use it to make the Nigerian red stew (page 12), efo riro (page 32), egusi (page 33), spicy black-eyed beans (page 43) and ewa agoyin (page 44).

OBE ATA
NIGERIAN RED SAUCE

MAKES 600ML

When I was growing up in Nigeria, the blenders weren't that powerful so there would always be someone in every neighbourhood who had a big grinder. You'd take your ingredients – your peppers, your tomatoes, your onions, your garlic – there so that they could blend them for you. We're not talking a little batch – it would be 25 litres of sauce at one time that they'd put in a bucket for you to take home, then you'd put it in the fridge or freezer. Nowadays everyone has a good blender, but back then, having that grinder was actually a business and you'd pay them to grind your ingredients for you. It was a big contraption that they'd also use to blend the beans to make moi moi (page 49) or to blend cassava skins to make what we call swallow – things like pounded yam, fufu or mashed potatoes.

1 red onion, roughly chopped

1 red pepper, roughly chopped

1 spring onion, roughly chopped

3 garlic cloves, roughly chopped

½ Scotch bonnet pepper

1 x 400g tin of plum tomatoes

50ml water (leave this out if making efo riro)

1 tbsp tomato purée

½ tsp ground ginger

½ tsp ground white pepper

Put everything in a blender or food processor (except the water if you're making efo riro, as you want that dish to be a bit thicker and coarser).

If you're making efo riro, pulse briefly, just until everything is roughly blended – you still want some texture.

If you're making this sauce to go with anything else, blend until smooth.

That's it! You're ready to use this as the base for all sorts of things now.

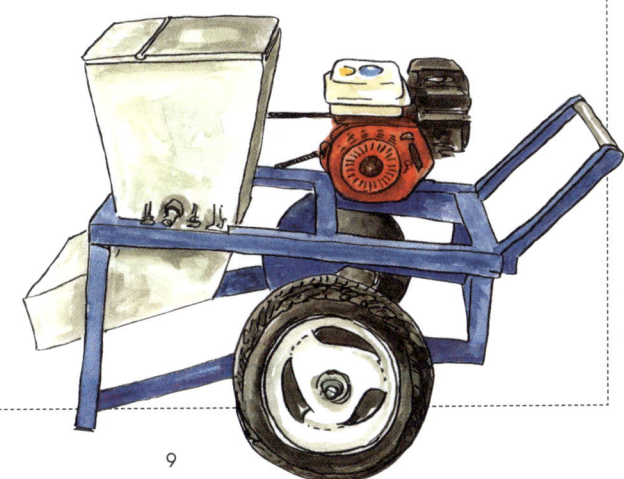

BROWN STEW CHICKEN

SERVES 4-6

There are variations of this dish all over the Caribbean, and everyone makes it a little bit differently. It's a stew that's in everyone's home, everyone's pot, every day. There would always be a pot of brown stew chicken simmering on the hob or some leftovers in the fridge. You come home from school and need something to eat? Brown stew chicken. Or you come home from work and can't think of what to make for dinner? Brown stew chicken. It's the answer to everything.

8 boneless, skinless chicken thighs

2 carrots, thinly sliced

2 spring onions, white and green parts thinly sliced

1 onion, diced

1 red pepper, diced

1 green pepper, diced

1 Scotch bonnet pepper

2 garlic cloves, crushed

3-4 bay leaves

1 large sprig of fresh thyme

3 tbsp ketchup

2 tbsp chicken bouillon or chicken seasoning

1 tsp ground ginger

1 tsp smoked paprika

1 tsp ground black pepper

½ tsp ground pimento (allspice)

3 tbsp dark brown sugar

500ml water

TO SERVE:

macaroni pie (page 54)

Put the chicken, veg, whole Scotch bonnet pepper, garlic, bay leaves, thyme and ketchup in a large bowl, then sprinkle over the bouillon or seasoning and the spices, tossing to coat. Cover with cling film and marinate in the fridge for at least 2 hours or overnight.

When you're ready to cook, put a large heavy-based saucepan on a medium heat. Add the sugar and let it melt and caramelise, stirring constantly – don't let it go too far and burn! If it does, start over, because burned sugar will make the whole dish bitter.

Add the chicken and vegetables, stirring to coat. The sugar will get very sticky, very fast, so add the hot water to loosen it. Scrape any hardened caramel off the spoon and back into the pan.

Bring to a boil, then reduce the heat, cover the pan and simmer for 45 minutes, until the chicken is cooked through and the veg are soft. Serve with a slice of macaroni pie on the side.

HOT TIP
If you're worried about the heat from a Scotch bonnet pepper – and they are HOT! – a good trick is to leave it whole and don't pierce the skin. That way, its flavour and a gentler heat infuse into the dish and you can remove it at the end.

SOCAFRO

NIGERIAN RED STEW

SERVES 4

Just like in Trinidad you'd always have a pot of brown stew chicken (page 10) on the go or in the fridge, in Nigeria you'd have a pot of red stew. You can put whatever meat or offal you want in this, but beef is the most common and it's what I use too. You can also serve it with whatever you like. It pairs really nicely with efo riro (page 32), yam (page 50), agege bread (page 57) or akara (page 46) for dipping – it goes with anything. But this beef stew served with jollof rice and fried plantain on the side is the ultimate combo. It's my perfect Sunday meal.

FOR THE SAUCE:
2 red peppers, chopped
1 red onion, chopped
6 garlic cloves, chopped
1 x 400g tin of plum tomatoes
a splash of water

FOR THE STEW:
500g diced beef (not stewing beef)
1 tbsp chicken bouillon
½ tsp ground black pepper
60ml vegetable oil
1 small onion, diced
salt and freshly ground black pepper

TO SERVE:
jollof rice (page 38)
fried plantain (page 52)

To make the sauce, put everything in a blender or food processor and blitz until smooth.

Put the beef in a bowl and sprinkle over the bouillon and black pepper. Set aside.

Heat the oil in a large saucepan over a medium-high heat. Add the onion and cook for about 5 minutes, stirring, until softened. Pour in the sauce. When it starts to bubble, add the beef and reduce the heat to medium. Cover the pan and cook for 30 minutes, stirring occasionally, until the beef is cooked through. Season to taste.

Serve with jollof rice and fried plantain on the side.

TRY THIS
If you have a batch of the obe ata (Nigerian red sauce) on page 9, you can use that instead of the sauce here.

SOCAFRO

NIGERIAN SUYA
SPICY BEEF SKEWERS

SERVES 1

Suya is a popular street food but you'd never see someone selling suya during the day. We only eat suya at night-time, like how you'd go out for a kebab after a few drinks with friends here. Or if you're out on a date and you go for a nice sit-down meal, you still might get some suya after. Even if the only place you go is to get suya, it's still a date!

My first secret to making suya is to find the best pepper mix that you can. It's a pre-made mix, also called yaji. I get mine directly from Nigeria. The second secret is that I use fillet, a premium cut of beef, so it's tender and not as dry as it would be if you use a cheaper cut.

One time I had a Nigerian customer come to my stall specifically to try my suya. He told me later that he'd asked where he could get suya in Waterford and someone had told him, 'The only person who does it is JD.' He'd never had any of my food and he didn't have high hopes but said he'd go try it anyway. So he came, bought some suya and went home. About an hour later, I got a call. He rang to tell me that it was phenomenal – that he'd never had suya made to such a high level, not even where he came from. It was a real taste of home for him. But that's the thing: I wouldn't put a dish on my menu if I couldn't make it to the same level – or better – as what we have in Nigeria.

350g beef fillet, cut into slices 5mm thick

80ml vegetable oil

3 tbsp suya pepper mix (see the intro)

1 tsp chicken bouillon (optional – use this if your suya mix doesn't already include salt)

TO SERVE:

thinly sliced red onion

thinly sliced tomatoes

fresh flat-leaf parsley leaves

Put the beef in a bowl with the oil, suya and bouillon (if using). Massage the oil and spices into the beef, then cover the bowl and marinate in the fridge for 3 hours.

When you're ready to cook, thread the beef onto skewers. Now this couldn't be easier. You can cook the beef on a baking tray under a hot grill or in an air fryer at 200°C for 10 minutes.

Serve with some thinly sliced raw red onion, tomatoes and a handful of parsley leaves. In Nigeria, this would all be wrapped up like a burrito in a sheet of newspaper and served as street food. You get back in your car or walk home and you open it up and the smell just hits you – it's fiery!

STUFFED PEPPERS

MAKES 4

This is what I cook when I feel like I need to have something healthy or light or a little bit different.

60ml vegetable oil

1 small onion, diced

500g beef mince

½ Scotch bonnet pepper

1 x 400g tin of plum tomatoes

1½ x 10g Maggi chicken stock cubes

1 tsp garlic powder

½ tsp ground ginger

½ tsp ground black pepper

a pinch of dried thyme

4 small red or yellow peppers

TO SERVE:

boiled rice or jollof rice (page 38)

Preheat the grill to high. Line a baking tray with foil or non-stick baking paper.

Heat the oil in a large frying pan over a medium heat. Add the onion and cook for about 10 minutes, stirring occasionally, until softened. Add the beef mince, breaking it up with the back of a spoon, and cook for 5–10 minutes, until browned. Add half a Scotch bonnet pepper, then stir in the tomatoes, crumble in the stock cubes and add the garlic powder, ginger, black pepper and thyme. Break up the tomatoes with the back of a spoon, then simmer for about 20 minutes, until the beef is cooked through, the tomatoes have reduced a bit and all the flavours have married together.

Meanwhile, cut the top off of each pepper and remove the inner core and seeds. Spoon the beef mixture into the hollowed-out peppers, then put them on the lined baking tray and pop them under the grill. Cook for about 10 minutes, turning regularly, until the peppers are soft and starting to blister.

Serve hot with boiled rice or jollof rice on the side.

TRY THIS
Stuff the peppers with jollof rice (page 38) instead of the beef mince.

SOCAFRO

JD'S JERK CHICKEN CURRY

SERVES 4

I developed this jerk chicken curry not only to suit the Irish palate (in other words, not too spicy), but also the Irish weather. Jerk is usually more of a thick paste that's slathered on meat and cooked on a barbecue, but let's be honest – you can't count on the weather co-operating for outdoor cooking here. So I wanted to make something that could be easily cooked indoors instead, especially for serving at my food stall. This jerk curry makes it foolproof. Served with jollof rice and fried plantain, it's the No. 1 bestseller at Socafro Kitchen.

2 bunches of spring onions, white and light green parts roughly chopped

2 fresh red chillies, roughly chopped, or ½ Scotch bonnet pepper

1 green pepper, chopped

1 small head of garlic, cloves peeled

3-4 sprigs of fresh thyme, leaves picked, or 1 tsp dried thyme

2 x 10g Maggi stock cubes

juice of 1 lemon

1 tbsp dark brown sugar

1 tbsp oil

1 tsp curry powder

1 tsp paprika

1 tsp ground pimento (allspice)

a splash of water, to blend

a pinch of fine sea salt

8 boneless, skinless chicken thighs or 4 chicken fillets

TO SERVE:

jollof rice (page 38) or rice and peas (page 41)

fried plantain (page 52)

This couldn't be easier. Just put everything except the chicken in a blender and blitz together, but try not to blend it so long that it's completely smooth – ideally, you want it to still have some texture. If you're using a smaller blender, like a Nutribullet, you'll need to do this in two batches.

If you want to make this ahead of time, you can add the chicken to the sauce and marinate it in the fridge overnight. Otherwise, pour the sauce into a large heavy-based saucepan or casserole. Add the chicken, stirring to coat. Bring to a boil, then reduce the heat to medium, cover the pan or casserole with a lid and cook for 1 hour. You want the sauce to reduce but not so much that it catches and burns, so stir occasionally and lower the heat if it's reducing too much. The chicken should be tender enough to shred easily with two forks. Check the seasoning.

Serve with jollof rice or rice and peas and some fried plantain on the side.

LOW & SLOW
Put the blended sauce and chicken in a slow cooker, cover with a lid and cook on low for 8 hours. The sauce won't reduce, but you could transfer everything to a large saucepan and reduce it on the hob if you want.

SOCAFRO

CHARMAINE'S CHICKEN SOUP WITH DUMPLINGS

SERVES 4-6

This is the first dish I ever learned how to make, when I was around eight years old. My older sister, Charmaine, taught it to me – Charmaine the Pain of Mulberry Lane, as I called her back then (sorry, sis!). I started by helping her to make the dumplings, which were my favourite part. They still are.

8 boneless, skinless chicken thighs, cut into bite-sized pieces

300g baby potatoes, halved lengthways

1 onion, diced

1 leek, halved lengthways and sliced into half-moons

1 whole Scotch bonnet pepper (optional)

2 litres chicken stock

1 tbsp chicken bouillon

1 tbsp coarsely ground black pepper

FOR THE DUMPLINGS:

350g plain flour

a pinch of salt

a handful of fresh flat-leaf parsley, finely chopped

200ml water

To make the stew, just put everything in a big saucepan and bring to a boil, then reduce the heat, cover the pan and simmer for 1–1½ hours.

To make the dumplings, whisk the flour and a pinch of salt together in a medium-sized bowl, then stir in the parsley, pour in the water and knead to bring it together into a soft dough.

Pinch off small balls of dough – about the size of a ping pong ball – and add to the stew. Cover the pan again and cook for another 15 minutes, until the dumplings are cooked through.

Season to taste and divide among bowls to serve.

SOCAFRO

SOCAFRO FRIED CHICKEN

MAKES 10 DRUMSTICKS

You've got some chicken and you want to make something quick, so you just season it well and fry it – no flour, no breadcrumbs – and have it with anything. My favourite combo, though, is with carnival rice and fried plantain.

10 chicken drumsticks

1 tbsp chicken bouillon

1 tbsp garlic powder

1 tsp onion powder

1 tsp ground black pepper

vegetable oil, for deep-frying

TO SERVE:

carnival rice (page 40)

fried plantain (page 52)

Put the chicken in a large bowl and sprinkle over the bouillon, garlic and onion powder and the black pepper. Massage the seasonings into the chicken. You can cook it right now, but if you have time, cover the bowl and put it in the fridge to marinate for at least 3 hours or overnight.

Heat the oil in a deep-fryer to 175°C.

Working in batches, add the chicken to the hot oil, making sure each drumstick is fully immersed. Fry for 12–15 minutes, until golden brown and fully cooked through – if you're unsure, the internal temperature should be 74°C (165°F) on an instant-read digital thermometer.

Serve hot with carnival rice and fried plantain on the side.

CREAMY COCONUT CHICKEN CURRY

SERVES 4-6

This dish is so popular at Socafro Kitchen that I had loads of customers asking me if it was going to be included in the book, so here you go!

TO MARINATE THE CHICKEN:

8 boneless, skinless chicken thighs (1.2kg)

1 tbsp chicken bouillon

1 tbsp garlic powder

1 tsp onion powder

1 tsp ground black pepper

FOR THE CURRY:

60ml vegetable oil

1 onion, diced

2 carrots, thinly sliced

1 red pepper, diced

1 green pepper, diced

1 sprig of fresh thyme

2 tsp curry powder

1 tsp ground turmeric

½ tsp ground ginger

2 x 400ml tins of coconut milk

TO SERVE:

rice and peas (page 41)

Put the chicken in a large bowl and sprinkle over the bouillon, garlic and onion powder and the black pepper. Massage the seasonings into the chicken. You can cook it right now, but if you have time, cover the bowl and put it in the fridge to marinate for at least 3 hours or overnight.

Heat the oil in a large saucepan over a medium heat. Add the onion, carrots, peppers, thyme, curry powder, turmeric and ginger and cook, stirring occasionally, for about 10 minutes, until the veg are softened.

Add the chicken and coconut milk and bring to a boil, then immediately reduce the heat and simmer for 30 minutes, until the chicken is cooked through.

Divide the curry among bowls and serve with rice and peas on the side.

MAKE IT VEGETARIAN

Use a tin of chickpeas, drained and rinsed, instead of the chicken, and vegetable bouillon instead of chicken bouillon.

NIGERIAN PEPPER SOUP

SERVES 4-6

If you've got a cold or you're feeling poorly, pepper soup is what you have. It will clear your sinuses and pick you back up. To make pepper soup, you need to get your hands on some pepper soup seasoning mix (not obe ata!). You can buy it in African or Arab shops.

50ml vegetable oil

1 onion, diced

8 boneless chicken thighs, ideally with the skin on (1.2kg)

1 Scotch bonnet pepper, left whole

2 litres chicken stock

1½ tbsp pepper soup seasoning mix (see the intro)

1 tsp crayfish seasoning

a pinch of garlic powder

a pinch of ground ginger

a pinch of ground white pepper

a pinch of ground black pepper

a handful of fresh flat-leaf parsley, leaves picked

Heat the oil in a large saucepan over a medium heat. Add the onion and cook for about 10 minutes, stirring occasionally, until softened.

Add the rest of the ingredients except the parsley and bring to a boil, then continue to boil on a high heat for about 45 minutes. Reduce the heat to medium and simmer for 15 minutes more.

Stir in the parsley leaves right at the end, then divide among bowls to serve.

SOCAFRO

BAKE & HAKE

SERVES 4

Bake and shark is practically the national dish of Trinidad. Shark isn't readily available in Ireland, so we have to use hake or cod instead. I guess that makes this bake and hake!

Battered, deep-fried shark meat is put inside a split fried bake with cucumber, tomato, red onion and lettuce, pineapple chutney, some tamarind sauce, pepper sauce and garlic mayo. It's so good that Andrew Zimmern, who hosted the TV show *Bizarre Eats*, called this the best sandwich he's ever eaten. If you ever go to Trinidad, try Richard's Bake and Shark on Maracas Beach.

500g skinned and deboned hake or cod fillets, cut into bite-sized pieces

juice of 1 lime

½–1 fresh red chilli (depending on how hot the chilli is), finely chopped

1 tbsp finely chopped mixed fresh herbs, such as coriander, parsley and thyme

1 tsp finely chopped garlic

1 tsp sea salt

freshly ground black pepper

vegetable oil, for deep-frying

100g plain flour

TO SERVE:

fried bake (page 56)

shredded lettuce

thinly sliced tomatoes

thinly sliced cucumbers

thinly sliced red onion

garlic mayo

pineapple, mango or tamarind chutney

hot sauce or pepper sauce

Make the fried bake as per the recipe on page 56.

After the fried bake dough has risen and just before you start to roll out the dough and cook it, put the hake or cod in a bowl and drizzle over the lime juice. Add the chilli, herbs, garlic, salt and a crack of pepper and toss to coat. Set aside to marinate while you fry the bake.

Heat the oil in your deep-fryer to 180°C. Fry the bake and keep it warm while you cook the fish.

Put the flour in a wide, shallow bowl and season it generously with salt and pepper. Dredge each piece of fish in the seasoned flour, making sure it's completely coated.

With the oil in the deep-fryer still at 180°C and working in batches, fry the fish for about 8 minutes in total, until it's cooked through, golden brown and crisp.

Tip the fried fish out onto a wire rack set over a baking tray lined with kitchen paper to let any excess oil drain off. Putting the fish on the rack instead of directly onto the kitchen paper will keep it crispy.

To serve, split a fried bake in half around the equator. Add a few pieces of fried fish to the bottom half, then pile on whatever toppings you'd like and sandwich together with the top half. Close your eyes, take a bite and imagine you're on Maracas Beach.

SOCAFRO

TRINI CURRIED PRAWNS WITH COCONUT RICE

SERVES 4

Prawns are expensive in Nigeria, so my mum would make this as a special occasion dish for a change from curried chicken or beef if we had family or other visitors coming over.

200g frozen king prawns, thawed

½ tsp ground black pepper

1 tbsp vegetable oil

1 tsp curry powder

1 small onion, diced

3 ripe tomatoes, diced

½ x 10g Maggi chicken stock cube, crumbled

a small handful of fresh flat-leaf parsley, chopped

TO SERVE:

Timea's coconut rice (page 42)

Make the coconut rice as per the recipe on page 42. When the cooking time is nearly done, sprinkle the king prawns with the ground black pepper and set aside.

Heat the vegetable oil in a frying pan over a medium heat, then add the curry powder and cook for just 30 seconds to infuse the oil. Add the onion, tomatoes and crumbled stock cube and cook for about 10 minutes, until the onion has softened and the tomatoes have broken down into a thick sauce.

Add the seasoned prawns and cook for about 3 minutes, just until they turn translucent, then stir in the parsley.

To serve, fluff up the coconut rice with a fork. Divide the rice among plates and spoon the curried prawns on top, trying to make sure the prawns are evenly shared out.

SOCAFRO

SOCAFRO SMOKED MACKEREL

SERVES 4-6

This is my version of salt fish in obe ata (Nigerian red sauce) because we can't readily get salt fish in Ireland (but check out the recipe for salt fish brandade in *Blasta Books 10: Whole Catch* to make it yourself). This is one of my mum's Caribbean recipes, but in Nigeria we never got salt fish either, so we always used freshly smoked mackerel that we'd get from the Sunday market and have this as our Sunday morning breakfast.

50ml vegetable oil (or enough to cover the surface of your pan)

3 medium red onions, diced

4 garlic cloves, chopped

3 ripe tomatoes, chopped

1 tsp curry powder

1 tsp chilli flakes

1 tsp crayfish seasoning

2-3 smoked mackerel fillets, skin and bones removed (300-450g)

sea salt and freshly ground black pepper

TO SERVE:

boiled or fried yam (page 50), fried bake (page 56) or eggs

Heat the oil in a medium-sized saucepan over a medium heat. Add the onions and cook, stirring occasionally, for about 10 minutes, until softened. Add the garlic and cook for 1 minute more, just until fragrant, then add the tomatoes, curry powder, chilli flakes and crayfish seasoning. Simmer for 10 minutes to bring the flavours together and to let the tomatoes soften and break down into a sauce.

Flake in the smoked mackerel and simmer for 5 minutes to heat through, then season to taste.

Serve with boiled or fried yam or fried bake. Or you can crack an egg in the pan and scramble it all together – or serve scrambled eggs separately, on the side – and that's tasty too.

SOCAFRO

EFO RIRO

SERVES 4-6

Efo riro is a traditional tomato and spinach stew that is usually served with what we call swallow - things like pounded yam, fufu, amala or semolina. These are thick, starchy foods that you swallow rather than chew, a bit like mashed potatoes here in Ireland. But my mum was never big on swallow, so we always had it with white rice and plantain and that would be a complete meal that we'd have once a week.

6 tbsp vegetable oil

1 small red onion, thinly sliced

1 batch of base obe ata (Nigerian red sauce, page 9)

sea salt and freshly ground black pepper

200ml vegetable stock

½ tsp crayfish seasoning

500g fresh spinach, roughly chopped

3 tbsp palm oil or vegetable oil

TO SERVE:

boiled rice or pounded yam (page 50)

Heat the oil in a large saucepan over a medium heat. Add the onion and cook for a few minutes to soften.

Pour in the obe ata (Nigerian red sauce) and cover the pan immediately with a lid or stand back because it will likely splatter. Simmer, uncovered, for 20 minutes, stirring occasionally, until the oil separates out and floats to the top. Season to taste with salt and pepper.

Add the stock and crayfish powder and simmer for 10–15 minutes more, until the oil separates out again.

To finish, stir in the spinach and oil to give it a nice shine. Reduce the heat and simmer gently for a final 10 minutes to wilt the spinach and bring it all together.

Divide the efo riro among bowls and serve with boiled rice or pounded yam.

TRY THIS
You can add any type of meat or fish to the efo riro or serve it alongside.

EGUSI

SERVES 4

This is similar to the efo riro on page 32 but it uses ground melon seeds (egusi), which you can get at Asian, Indian or African shops. Nigerians love it but so does everyone who tries it. Timea, my Hungarian wife, can't get enough of it and when I brought a friend of mine from the States with me to Nigeria one time, this was his No. 1 dish. When it was a cold day, my mum would serve this with pounded yam (although a 'cold' day in Nigeria is like 20°C or 25°C).

8 tbsp palm oil or vegetable oil

1 small red onion, thinly sliced

1 batch of obe ata (Nigerian red sauce, page 9)

200g egusi (ground melon seeds)

4 tbsp hot water

200ml vegetable stock

½ tsp crayfish seasoning

1-2 handfuls of fresh spinach, roughly chopped

sea salt and freshly ground black pepper

TO SERVE:
boiled rice or pounded yam (page 50)

Heat the oil in a large saucepan over a medium heat. Add the onion and cook for a few minutes to soften. Stir in the obe ata (Nigerian red sauce), cover the pan with a lid and simmer for 20 minutes, until the oil separates out and floats to the top.

Mix the egusi (ground melon seeds) and hot water in a small bowl until it forms a paste, then stir this into the pan along with the vegetable stock and crayfish seasoning. Cover and simmer for another 10–15 minutes.

Stir in the spinach and allow it to wilt, then season to taste with salt and pepper.

Divide the egusi among bowls and serve with boiled rice or pounded yam.

YAM & EGGS

SERVES 2-4

You know the way we always have a bag of potatoes in the house in Ireland? In Nigeria, we always have yam. We'd have yam and eggs a lot for breakfast before school because yam is filling, just like the way you're going to feel full if you eat a lot of potatoes.

2 tbsp vegetable oil

1 red onion, halved and thinly sliced

1 spring onion, green and white parts thinly sliced

1 small ripe tomato, diced

a pinch of chicken bouillon

a pinch of curry powder

a pinch of ground black pepper

4 eggs, beaten

a knob of butter

TO SERVE:

boiled yam (page 50)

Heat the oil in a small saucepan over a medium heat. Add the red onion, spring onion and tomato along with the chicken bouillon, curry powder and black pepper. Cook for about 10 minutes, until softened.

Push the veg to the sides of the pan and reduce the heat to low. Pour the beaten eggs into the centre of the pan and cook for a few minutes, stirring constantly with a spatula or wooden spoon to softly scramble them. Once the eggs are done, stir in the veg to mix everything together and add the knob of butter to finish.

Serve straightaway with boiled yam alongside.

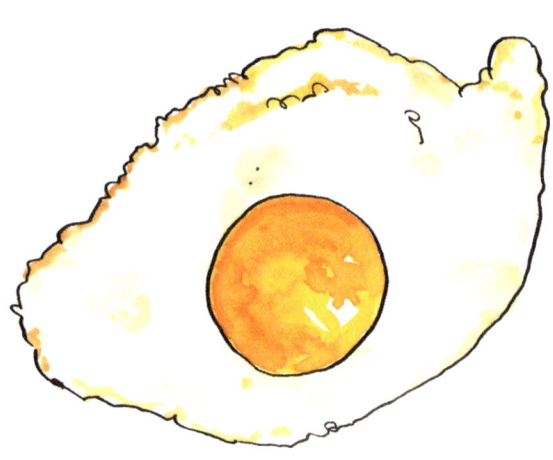

INDOMIE & EGGS

SERVES 2

Indomie is a brand of ramen noodles but we call this dish by that brand name, no matter what kind we use, and we take our time to make it nice. Just pouring hot water into a Pot Noodle like we do in Ireland? No way!

Kids love Indomie and eggs – it's every child's favourite – and we survive on Indomie as students at university. It's even sold as street food. There are guys who sell it with eggs, with agege bread (page 57) or with coffee. Everyone makes it and everyone loves it.

2 packs of Indomie chicken ramen, including the seasoning packets

3 tbsp vegetable oil

6-8 king prawns, thawed if frozen (optional)

1 small onion, diced

1 small red pepper, diced

1 small green pepper, diced

1 tomato, deseeded and diced

½ Scotch bonnet pepper, finely diced (optional - if using the Indomie brand, check to see if there is already chilli powder in the mix that comes with it and omit the Scotch bonnet if so)

½ tsp curry powder

2 tbsp water

3 eggs

a pinch of chicken bouillon

Cook the noodles as per the packet instructions. Drain.

Meanwhile, heat the oil in a large frying pan over a medium heat. Add the prawns (if using) and cook for 3 minutes, just until they turn translucent. Set aside.

Add the veg, Scotch bonnet (if using), curry powder, water and just one packet of the ramen seasoning to the pan. Cook for about 10 minutes, until the onion and peppers have softened and the tomato has broken down.

Add the drained noodles to the pan and toss to combine, then push everything to the sides of the pan. Beat one egg in a small bowl, then add it to the centre of the pan with a pinch of bouillon. Allow to cook until the bottom is firm, then break it up with a spatula and stir it into the ramen. Add the prawns back to the pan to heat through again.

In a separate pan, fry the remaining two eggs to your liking.

To serve, divide the ramen between two plates and add a fried egg on top of each one.

BE CAREFUL!
Wear plastic gloves to dice the Scotch bonnet – you do NOT want to accidentally rub your eyes after handling this pepper!

JOLLOF RICE

SERVES 6-8

It's not a Nigerian party if jollof rice isn't being served. And because it's a party food, there's no such thing as a small pot of jollof rice – we're talking about serving 200 or 300 people, so it's cooked outside over an open fire.

Jollof rice can be a dish on its own or you can have it with fried chicken (page 22), beef or coleslaw, but because it's cooked right in the sauce, you don't really need to pair it with much. At my stall, I serve it with jerk chicken curry (page 18).

Jollof rice is originally from Senegal but Nigerians and Ghanaians have also claimed it as their own, so there's always a big rivalry between who has the best jollof rice. Everyone has their own version of jollof rice and everyone says they cook it better. Customers even ask me if the jollof rice I make at my stall is Nigerian jollof or Ghanaian jollof. I tell them it's JD's jollof.

FOR THE SAUCE:

2 red peppers, roughly chopped

1 red onion, roughly chopped

1 Scotch bonnet pepper, halved

6 garlic cloves, roughly chopped

100ml water

1 tbsp tomato purée

FOR THE RICE:

250ml vegetable oil

1 tsp dried thyme

½ tsp curry powder

½ tsp ground ginger

2 tbsp tomato purée

750g basmati rice

2½ x 10g Maggi chicken stock cubes (or 5 x 4g cubes)

To make the sauce, put everything in a blender or food processor and blitz until smooth.

To make the rice, heat the oil in a large heavy-based pot or casserole over a medium heat. Add the thyme, curry powder and ginger and cook for just 30 seconds to infuse the oil, then add the tomato purée and cook for 1–2 minutes more.

Pour in the sauce, stirring to incorporate the oil. Cover with a tight-fitting lid and simmer for about 30 minutes, until the colour of the sauce deepens and the oil separates out and floats on top.

Stir in the rice and crumble in the stock cubes, then reduce the heat to medium-low. Cover the pan tightly with a sheet of foil, then cover that with the lid. Cook for 30–40 minutes to gently cook the rice in the sauce.

Now if you want to give your jollof rice a smoky flavour, crank up the heat full blast with the pot still covered and let the bottom of the rice burn (don't do this if you're using your best or your favourite pot!). The smoke will permeate through the rest of the rice – just don't eat that bottom burned layer.

When it's done, fluff up the rice with a fork and serve.

SOCAFRO

CARNIVAL RICE

SERVES 4-6

This is my version of Nigerian fried rice with a Caribbean twist. It's also completely different from Chinese fried rice because we don't mix egg into it. Like jollof rice, you'll often get fried rice at parties. Both will often be served, so you'll get one scoop of jollof rice and one scoop of fried rice – they go hand in hand.

500g basmati rice

1 litre vegetable stock

2 bay leaves

1 tsp ground turmeric

50ml vegetable oil

300g frozen mixed vegetables, thawed

2 spring onions, thinly sliced

½ tsp dried thyme

sea salt and freshly ground black pepper

Put the rice, stock, bay leaves and turmeric in a large heavy-based saucepan set over a high heat and bring to a boil, then reduce the heat to medium-low, cover with a tight-fitting lid and cook for about 15 minutes, until all the stock has been absorbed.

Meanwhile, heat the oil in a frying pan over a medium heat. Add the mixed veg, spring onions and thyme and cook for a few minutes, until the spring onions have softened and the vegetables are heated through but have still kept their bright colours. Season to taste.

When the rice is done, fluff it up with a fork and gently stir in the veg. Serve alongside meat or fish. I sometimes add a 250g bag of frozen prawns, like in the coconut rice recipe on page 42, and eat a big bowl of this just on its own.

RICE & PEAS

SERVES 4-6

At Socafro Kitchen, I usually make this with rice and kidney beans, but in Trinidad we make it with gungo peas (aka pigeon peas). Just as jollof rice is such an important dish in Nigeria, rice and peas is the same in the Caribbean. It's an everyday dish that we have with everything, but it's also a complete protein if you eat it on its own.

600g basmati rice

1 x 400g tin of gungo peas (aka pigeon peas) or kidney beans, drained and rinsed

1 x 400ml tin of coconut milk

400ml chicken or vegetable stock

1 spring onion, cut into thirds

1 sprig of fresh thyme

This couldn't be easier. Just put everything in a large saucepan and bring to a boil, then cover the pan with a lid, reduce the heat to medium-low and simmer for 12–15 minutes, until all the liquid has been absorbed. Fluff up the rice with a fork and you're done.

TIMEA'S COCONUT RICE

SERVES 4–6

My wife Timea is Hungarian but she makes coconut rice better than I do! Maybe it should actually be called Timea's Afro-Caribbean-Hungarian coconut rice. It's become her signature dish now and is a family favourite.

2 tbsp vegetable oil

500g basmati rice

300g frozen mixed veg, thawed

1 x 250g bag of tiny prawns, thawed if frozen

600ml chicken stock

1 x 400ml tin of coconut milk

1 tsp curry powder

½ tsp ground turmeric

Heat the oil in a large heavy-based saucepan over a medium heat. Add the rice and cook for a few minutes, stirring, just until it turns a bit translucent. Add the veg, prawns, stock, coconut milk, curry powder and turmeric. Bring to a boil, then reduce the heat to medium-low, cover the pan and cook for 12–15 minutes, until all the liquid has been absorbed into the rice. Remove the pan from the heat and keep covered.

To serve, fluff up the coconut rice with a fork.

SPICY BLACK-EYED BEANS

SERVES 4-6

This was a typical weekday breakfast that we'd normally have with agege bread (page 57). It's basically Nigerian beans on toast. When my older sister makes this, she adds a spoonful of sugar as a secret ingredient.

1 batch of obe ata (Nigerian red sauce, page 9)

2 x 400g tins of black-eyed beans, drained and rinsed

500ml water

2 tbsp vegetable bouillon

½ tbsp onion powder

1 tsp ground black pepper

TO SERVE:

agege bread (page 57), fried bake (page 56) or boiled rice

Make the obe ata (Nigerian red sauce) on page 9 as per the instructions for the efo riro, blending it until smooth.

Meanwhile, put the drained beans in a saucepan with the water and bring to a boil, then reduce the heat and simmer for 10–15 minutes. Even though the beans are tinned and are therefore already cooked, we're cooking them further here to get them nice and soft.

Add the blended sauce along with the bouillon, onion powder and ground black pepper. Simmer for 20–30 minutes more, until it's nice and thick.

Serve with agege bread or fried bake for scooping up the beans. This is also good with boiled rice.

EWA AGOYIN

SERVES 4-6

This is similar to the spicy black-eyed beans on page 43, but the big difference is the way you serve it: you put the sauce on top of the boiled beans rather than mixing everything together like you do with the spicy beans. Another way it's different is that the sauce in ewa agoyin is a lot more reduced, almost burnt, and the beans are mashed. And whereas the spicy beans is an everyday dish, we'd never make ewa agoyin at home because we'd buy it as street food. Women who came from the neighbouring country, the Republic of Benin, would make this dish and sell it on the roadsides in Lagos. They'd carry it in big pans on their heads.

FOR THE SAUCE:

1 batch of obe ata (Nigerian red sauce, page 9)

100ml vegetable oil

2 ripe tomatoes, deseeded and diced

1 red onion, halved and thinly sliced

1 small red pepper, diced

FOR THE BEANS:

4 x 400g tins of black-eyed beans, drained and rinsed

500ml water

3 tbsp vegetable bouillon powder

1 tbsp onion powder

1 tbsp crayfish seasoning

sea salt and freshly ground black pepper

TO SERVE:

agege bread (page 57) or fried bake (page 56)

Make the obe ata (Nigerian red sauce) as per the instructions on page 9 for efo riro, blending it until smooth.

Heat the oil in a large saucepan over a medium heat. Add the tomatoes, onion and pepper and cook for 5 minutes, until starting to soften, then pour in the blended sauce and simmer, uncovered, for 30–40 minutes, until it's really reduced.

Meanwhile, put the drained beans in a separate saucepan with the water, bouillon, onion powder and crayfish seasoning and bring to a boil, then reduce the heat and simmer for 10–15 minutes. Even though the beans are tinned and are already cooked, we're cooking them further here to get them nice and soft. Mash them with the back of the ladle, then season to taste with salt and pepper.

To serve, divide the mashed beans among bowls and ladle some of the sauce on top. Serve with agege bread or fried bake for scooping everything up.

TRY THIS

Here's a different way to use the pepper sauce that you make in this ewa agoyin. Preheat the oven to 200°C (180°C fan). Line a baking tray with foil. Peel four to six ripe plantains (one per person) and put them on the lined tray in a single layer. Bake in the preheated oven for 30–40 minutes, checking after 30 minutes, until they are all nicely browned and softened. Cut each one in half lengthways and split it open. To serve, spoon the pepper sauce down the middle, almost as if the roasted plantain was a baked potato.

SOCAFRO

AKARA
NIGERIAN BEAN FRITTERS

MAKES APPROX. 24

Akara are bean fritters that are traditionally made by soaking dried black-eyed beans in water, getting rid of all the skins, then blending the soaked beans into a paste, but using bean flour makes them so much easier.

Akara are a popular street food snack. You could buy a few to eat them on their own, but we'd often eat akara with ogi (also called pap), a type of custard made from corn with added sugar and evaporated milk. It's a lovely combination, especially because sometimes akara can be a little dry. You can get the special fermented corn flour to make ogi in Arab or African shops – look for the words ogi, akamu, pap or koko on the packaging – or try eating the akara with a European style of custard.

230g ewa flour (bean flour)

375ml warm water

½ onion, roughly chopped

½ red pepper, roughly chopped

½ Scotch bonnet pepper, roughly chopped (see the tip on page 35)

50ml cold water

1 tsp crayfish seasoning (optional)

a pinch of ground white pepper

a pinch of ground black pepper

vegetable oil, to deep-fry

Mix the bean flour and warm water together in a large bowl until it's a thick batter with a dropping consistency. Cover the bowl and set aside for 30 minutes.

Put the onion, peppers, cold water, crayfish seasoning (if using) and white and black pepper in a blender and blitz until smooth, then add this to the rested batter. If it looks too runny, add a little more bean flour. It should be a dropping consistency, similar to puff-puff (page 60).

Heat the oil in a deep-fryer to 175°C.

Working in batches, carefully drop spoonfuls of the batter into the hot oil. Cook for 5–8 minutes, until puffed up, golden brown and cooked through. Drain on kitchen paper to absorb any excess oil. Eat warm.

SOCAFRO

MOI MOI
NIGERIAN STEAMED BEAN PUDDING

SERVES 4-6

Moi moi is one of those foods that you either like or you don't. There isn't really a middle ground. I think it's a texture thing – it's a smooth steamed pudding and I'm never sure what to compare it to to help people understand it. It's normally wrapped up and steamed in banana leaves and served that way. Traditionally, it's a little time-consuming to make because you'd have to soak, shell and blend your black-eyed beans or honey beans, but using bean flour is a quick shortcut. But if you want to make it the more traditional way, soak 2 cups of dried beans overnight, then peel off the skins by rubbing the beans between your fingers. Add the peeled beans to the blender or food processor and continue as per the method. Even better, look for bags of peeled dried beans in African shops so that you can just soak them and skip the peeling.

oil or butter, for greasing

4-5 eggs

4 cups ewa flour (bean flour)

2 red peppers, roughly chopped

1 white onion, roughly chopped

1 red onion, roughly chopped

½ Scotch bonnet pepper

125ml palm oil or vegetable oil

100ml water

2 tsp crayfish seasoning

1 tsp paprika

a pinch of garlic powder

a pinch of ground ginger

a pinch of ground white pepper

sea salt and freshly ground black pepper

TO SERVE:

jollof rice (page 38) or carnival rice (page 40)

Preheat the oven to 200°C (180°C fan). Grease 8–10 ramekins with a little oil or butter.

To hard-boil the eggs, put them in a medium saucepan and add enough cold water to cover them by about 1cm. Bring the water to a boil, then reduce the heat to a simmer and cook for 7 minutes. As soon as the eggs are cooked, drain and cool them rapidly under cold running water before peeling and cutting in half lengthways. (You can boil the eggs ahead of time and keep them in the fridge, unpeeled.)

Put everything else in a blender or food processor and blitz until it's a smooth, thick batter. Divide the batter among the greased ramekins, then add one half of a hard-boiled egg on top of each one, cut side facing up.

Put the ramekins in a roasting tin and pour in enough water to come halfway up the sides of the ramekins, then cover the top of the tin with a sheet of foil. Bake in the preheated oven for 30 minutes, then remove the foil and bake for 5 minutes more to brown the tops. They're done when a skewer inserted into the middle comes out clean.

Serve warm with jollof rice or carnival rice on the side.

HOW TO MAKE
YAM THREE WAYS

When you buy a yam, always ask the shop to cut it open for you to check that it's not rotten because you can't tell just by looking at it. There is nothing worse than making a special trip to get yam and needing it for a recipe, only to realise once you get home that it's bad. I speak from experience!

BOILED YAM

Cut away the tough outer skin of the yam, trying to keep as close to the skin as possible to avoid waste. Cut into slices, then rinse to get rid of the excess starch.

Put the yam in a pot of water with 4 teaspoons of caster sugar and 2 teaspoons of salt and bring to a boil, then reduce the heat a bit and simmer for 25–30 minutes, until soft. Drain and it's now ready to serve.

POUNDED YAM

Get a bag of yam flour and follow the packet instructions – all you have to do is add boiling water. Traditionally, though, you'd make pounded yam by literally pounding boiled yams in a huge pestle and mortar. In restaurants, it would take a big guy like me to do this – the pestle could be five feet long! The texture and taste when it's done by hand are so much better – and it's still made this way in smaller villages – but what you lose in taste, you gain in convenience.

FRIED YAM

Cut away the tough outer skin of the yam, trying to keep as close to the skin as possible to avoid waste. Cut the peeled yam into slices about 2.5cm thick, then cut into batons, like chips. Rinse the batons to get rid of the excess starch, then pat dry.

Heat some vegetable oil in a deep-fryer to 170°C (or pour a 2cm-deep layer of oil into a saucepan).

Put the batons in a large bowl and toss with a generous pinch of salt to coat. Depending on how big your yam is or how much you're cooking, you may need to work in batches, but you can cook more yam batons at a time than you would if you were cooking chips made from potatoes.

Add the batons to the hot oil and deep-fry for about 30 minutes (yes, that's 30 minutes), until light golden and starting to crisp up. The fried yam won't get a deep golden brown like potatoes, so don't be tempted to keep cooking it. Drain on kitchen paper to absorb any excess oil and it's ready to serve.

FRIED PLANTAIN

When I was a kid, I had fried plantain all the time as a snack. Green, unripe plantains are fried and sold as crisps, like potatoes are here in Ireland. These days I like to have fried plantain for breakfast with eggs or white rice, alongside jollof rice (page 38) or with any rice dish, really.

ripe plantains (see the tip)

vegetable oil, for deep-frying

Peel a ripe plantain and cut it into slices at an angle.

Heat some vegetable oil in a deep-fryer to 180°C.

Working in batches, add the plantain slices and deep-fry for a few minutes, until golden. Drain on kitchen paper to absorb any excess oil. You could dust the fried plantain with the cinnamon sugar from the puff-puff on page 60 if you want.

TOP TIP
Very ripe plantains are a blackish-yellow colour and soft – and the blacker the plantain is, the better, as it means it will be sweeter.

SOCAFRO

MACARONI PIE

SERVES 4-6

This was my favourite dish growing up. When my mum said she was making macaroni pie, there would be excitement galore - I'd start dancing! It's also one of the first dishes I learned how to cook (that and the fried bake on page 56).

This dish is different from the mac 'n' cheese you might be used to, because this version is baked until it's solid and you can cut it into slices. You know how we have potatoes on the side of the plate in Ireland? In Trinidad, we have a little slice of macaroni pie. You could have it on its own, but we'd have it on the side with some rice and peas (page 41), brown stew chicken (page 10) or steamed veg.

When I started Socafro Kitchen, macaroni pie was one of the first dishes I made and I'd give customers a really generous slice. These days I only serve it now and then, but it still has loyal fans.

1 tsp fine sea salt

500g macaroni

100g butter, plus extra for greasing

1 small onion, grated

3 eggs, beaten

2 x 410ml tins of evaporated milk

2 tbsp ketchup (optional)

1 tbsp chicken bouillon

1 tsp yellow mustard

1 tsp garlic powder

¾ tsp ground white pepper

½ tsp dried thyme

½ tsp cayenne pepper

2 x 250g packs of grated Cheddar and mozzarella cheese mix

Preheat the oven to 200°C (180°C fan). Grease a large baking dish – a lasagne dish would be perfect.

Bring a large saucepan of water to a boil with the teaspoon of salt. Add the pasta and cook it according to the packet instructions, until it's al dente. Drain and put the pasta back in the pot along with the butter. Let the butter melt, then stir to coat the pasta.

Put the grated onion, eggs, evaporated milk, ketchup (if using), chicken bouillon, mustard, garlic powder, white pepper, thyme and cayenne in a large mixing bowl and whisk to combine. Stir in one bag of the grated cheese, then add the cooked pasta and stir again.

Pour the macaroni into the greased baking dish and sprinkle the rest of the cheese on top. Bake in the preheated oven for 40–45 minutes, until golden brown, bubbling and set firm. Check it after 30 minutes and if the top is browning too much, cover it with foil.

Allow to stand for 10–15 minutes before cutting into slices to serve.

SOCAFRO

FRIED BAKE

MAKES 14-16

Variations of this bread are made all over the Caribbean. In Trinidad we call this fried bake, but in Jamaica it's called johnny cakes. If you roll up the dough into a cigar shape and fry it, then it's called festival in Jamaica. Or if you stuff the disc of bread with mashed potatoes before you fry it, it's called aloo pie, which reflects the Indian influence in Trinidad.

Fried bake goes well with so many things. It's often served with salt fish in the Caribbean but I like to have it with the smoked mackerel on page 30, the ewa agoyin (page 44) or spicy black-eyed beans (page 43) or with scrambled eggs for breakfast.

480g plain flour, plus extra for dusting

50g caster sugar

1 tbsp baking powder

2 x 7g sachets of fast-action dried yeast

60g butter, diced

150-175ml lukewarm water

vegetable oil, for deep-frying

Put the flour, sugar, baking powder and yeast in a large bowl and whisk to combine. Add the diced butter and rub it into the dry ingredients with your fingertips until the mixture resembles coarse breadcrumbs.

Slowly and gradually add the water, mixing and kneading it in by hand as you go. You might not need all the water or you might need a little more – you want just enough to bring everything together into a dough. Knead until smooth, then cover the bowl with a clean, damp tea towel and leave it in a warm place to rise for about 1 hour, until doubled in size.

Lightly dust a countertop with flour. Punch down the dough to knock the air out, then tip it out onto the countertop and knead until smooth. Pinch off golf ball-sized portions.

Heat some vegetable oil in a deep-fryer to 180°C. Alternatively, pour 2cm of oil into a large frying pan set on a medium-low heat and let it get hot.

While the oil heats up, roll out each ball into a circle with a floured rolling pin. Working in batches, add a few discs to the hot oil. Fry for 60–90 seconds, until they have puffed up and are golden brown on the bottom. Carefully turn them over and fry the other side for 60–90 seconds more, until golden brown all over.

Remove the fried bake with a slotted spoon and drain on kitchen paper to absorb any excess oil. These are best eaten while still warm and flaky.

AGEGE BREAD

MAKES 1 LOAF

Agege bread gets its name from Agege, a suburb of Lagos - it's actually the area where I grew up. It's our local bread, like a Waterford blaa is a local bread here in Ireland, but all Nigerians know and love agege bread. It was actually created by a Jamaican immigrant, Amos Shackleton, called 'the bread king of Nigeria'. Amos invented a tool called a dough break that created the bread's soft, pillowy texture. It's sweet, soft and baked in instantly recognisable rectangular loaves. It's a taste of home for any Nigerian.

280ml milk

125g caster sugar

1 x 7g sachet of fast-action dried yeast

500g strong white flour, plus extra for dusting

1 tsp sea salt

50g butter, diced and softened, plus extra for greasing

1 egg, beaten (optional)

Gently heat the milk just until it's lukewarm. Pour it into a jug, then stir in a spoonful of the sugar and sprinkle the yeast on top. Let it sit for 10 minutes, until the yeast has activated and has become frothy.

Put the remaining sugar in the bowl of a stand mixer fitted with the dough hook and add the flour and salt. Mix to combine, then add the diced butter and rub it in with your fingertips until the mixture resembles coarse breadcrumbs. Pour in the milk mixture, then knead on a low speed for 10 minutes, until it all comes together into a soft, elastic dough. You may need to add a little more flour if the dough is too sticky. (Alternatively, you can mix and knead all the ingredients together by hand.)

Form the dough into a ball, then cover the bowl with cling film. Put it in a warm, draught-free place for 1½ hours, until the dough has doubled in size.

Grease a 900g (2lb) loaf tin with butter. Punch down the dough to knock out the air, then tip it out onto a lightly floured work surface. Knead it briefly and form it into a log that will fit your loaf tin. Put it in the greased tin, cover loosely with a clean tea towel and put in a warm, draught-free place to rise again for about 1 hour, just until the dough has risen to the top of the tin.

Preheat the oven to 220°C (200°C fan).

Brush the top of the dough with the beaten egg (if using) for a nice shiny finish, then bake in the preheated oven for 45 minutes, until the top is golden brown and the bottom of the loaf sounds hollow when you turn it out of the tin and tap the bottom.

Allow to cool on a wire rack before cutting into slices to serve.

AUNTIE ANGELA'S COCONUT BAKE

MAKES 1 LARGE LOAF

The first time my wife, Timea, had coconut bake, we were staying with my auntie in Tobago in her beautiful house up in the hills. We'd had an incredible meal the night before, and that morning, coconut bake and salt fish were on the table for breakfast. 'That coconut bake tastes good, doesn't it?' I asked Timea, then looked up and saw there were tears in her eyes! She said she'd never tasted anything as good as that combination of the coconut bake and salt fish before. This is my Auntie Angela's recipe and take it from Timea, it's amazing.

550g plain flour, plus extra for dusting

1 x 7g sachet of fast-action dried yeast

2 tbsp light brown sugar

1½ tsp baking powder

1½ tsp sea salt

½ tsp ground nutmeg

55g cold butter, diced

1 x 400ml tin of coconut milk

Put the flour, yeast, sugar, baking powder, salt and nutmeg in a large bowl and whisk to combine. Add the diced butter and rub it into the dry ingredients with your fingertips until the mixture resembles coarse breadcrumbs.

Slowly and gradually add the coconut milk, mixing and kneading it in by hand as you go to bring everything together into a soft, sticky dough. (Or you could do this in a stand mixer fitted with a dough hook.) Knead for about 5 minutes, until smooth, then cover the bowl with a clean, damp tea towel and leave it in a warm place to rise for about 1 hour, until doubled in size.

Preheat the oven to 200°C (180°C fan). Line a 25cm cake tin or cast iron pan with non-stick baking paper and grease the paper with some butter.

Lightly dust a countertop with flour. Punch down the dough to knock the air out, then tip it out onto the countertop and knead briefly into a smooth ball. Transfer to the tin or pan and prick the top all over with the tines of a fork.

Bake in the preheated oven for 45–50 minutes, until nicely risen and golden brown. A skewer inserted into the centre should come out clean.

Allow to cool on a wire rack, then cut into wedges to serve.

SOCAFRO

CINNAMON PUFF-PUFF

MAKES 16-20

Puff-puff is a Nigerian street food. You'll find someone selling it on every street corner or along the side of a road. Walking home from school, you're gonna buy at least one or two. I think it's the No. 1 snack in Nigeria. Everyone loves puff-puff.

200g plain flour

70g caster or granulated sugar

1 x 7g sachet of fast-action dried yeast

½ tsp ground nutmeg

160ml lukewarm water

vegetable oil, for deep-frying

FOR THE CINNAMON SUGAR:

100g caster or granulated sugar

2 tbsp ground cinnamon

Put the flour, sugar, yeast and nutmeg in a large bowl and whisk to combine, then pour in the water and mix until it's a thick batter. Cover the bowl with a clean tea towel and let it rest in a warm place for about 30 minutes, until it's started to rise a little.

Meanwhile, put the sugar and cinnamon in a blender or food processor and blitz to a fine consistency.

Heat the oil in a deep-fryer to 180°C.

Working in batches, drop spoonfuls of the batter into the hot oil. Dip your spoon into a jug of hot water in between spoonfuls to clean it each time so the batter doesn't stick.

The batter should sink when you add it to the hot oil, then immediately bob back up to the surface. Cook for a few minutes, until light golden brown all over and puffed up, turning to let them cook on all sides. The puff-puff should be about the size of golf balls when cooked.

Briefly drain on kitchen paper to absorb any excess oil, then dust the puff-puff with the cinnamon sugar and eat while they're still warm.

PUFF-PUFF AROUND THE WORLD

Versions of this recipe – which is basically just fried dough balls – exist all over the world, with different names in different countries. Even in Ireland, Myrtle Allen had a similar recipe and called it Ballymaloe balloons. Some put honey in them, soak them in syrup or add raisins, while others just dust them with icing sugar. I'd only ever had plain puff-puff in Nigeria but I wanted to pair them with something, so I make mine with cinnamon sugar to give them a little twist.

Beignet in Cameroon, the Gambia and Senegal

Bofloto in the Ivory Coast

Bofrot in Ghana

Bolinho in Angola

Boortsog in Central Asia, Idel-Ural, the Middle East and Mongolia

Botokoin in Togo

Buñuelo in Spain and Latin America

Gato in Guinea and Mali

Gulab jamun in India, Pakistan, Bangladesh and Nepal

Kala in Liberia

Legemat in Sudan

Lockmaw in Turkey

Loukoumades in Greece

Mikate in Congo

Oliebol in the Netherlands

Vetkoek, amagwinya or magwinya in South Africa and Zimbabwe

Zeppole in Italy

NO-CHURN LEMON-LIME ICE CREAM

MAKES 1 LITRE

All these ingredients – lemons, limes, condensed milk, Angostura bitters – are things we use in a lot of our drinks in the Caribbean, so I wanted to see how they worked together in an ice cream. And let me tell you, they work great! It's sweet, it's sharp, it's sour – very refreshing and perfect for summer. You don't even need an ice cream maker for this and it still turns out smooth and creamy because of the condensed milk. It's a no-churn no-brainer.

2 lemons, quartered

3 limes, quartered

500ml water

2 x 400g tins of condensed milk

500ml double cream

3 dashes of Angostura bitters

1 tsp ground nutmeg

a handful of ice

Put the lemons, limes and water in a high-speed blender or food processor and blitz them, skins and all, until smooth. Pour into a jug through a fine mesh sieve to strain out the solids.

Put the strained lemon-lime mixture back in the blender or food processor with the rest of the ingredients and blend again until creamy and smooth.

Pour into a 1-litre airtight freezerproof container and cover. Freeze overnight – it will be softly frozen, not rock hard.

SOCAFRO

BLASTA BOOKS #12

A SHORT HISTORY OF
ANGOSTURA BITTERS

Did you know that Angostura bitters are only made in Trinidad? If you like cocktails, chances are you've been having a taste of Trinidad all this time and didn't even know it.

The bitters recipe itself has been a secret for 200 years. When the bitters were first produced in 1824, they were used as a medicinal tonic to alleviate stomach ailments for soldiers. (The company also says the bitters work as a mosquito repellent and a stain for porous surfaces.) It was only when the founder's three sons moved from their hometown of Angostura, Venezuela, to Trinidad that bitters started to be used as an ingredient in cocktails and food.

By the 1850s, the bitters were being exported around the Caribbean and to the US and UK. By the time of the Golden Age of the Cocktail in the 1900s, bitters' popularity was cemented as a key ingredient in classic cocktails such as old-fashioneds, Manhattans and whiskey sours.

Bitters are also commonly used in both sweet and savoury cooking in Trinidad (like in my lemon-lime ice cream on page 62). We add a dash of bitters as naturally as you'd add salt or pepper. No house should be without a bottle.

FROM ERROR TO ICONIC

I bet you've seen a bottle of Angostura bitters, with its yellow cap and oversized paper label, in bars or off-licences and never thought much about it. That label is iconic now, but it was actually a mistake.

To make a long story short, one brother in the company was in charge of the bottles and another brother was in charge of the labels, and they didn't consult each other. With no time to fix the problem before entering the bottle into a competition, the oversized label had to be used. They lost the competition, but the accidental branding has been used ever since.

SORREL

MAKES 1.5 LITRES

This is practically the national drink of Trinidad. It's always served at Christmas but also throughout the year. Funnily enough, this same drink is also made in Nigeria, where it's called zobo. With my Afro-Caribbean background, if I was a drink, I would be this one.

50g dried hibiscus flowers	Rinse the dried flowers in a fine mesh sieve, then put them in a saucepan with the water, cloves, bay leaves, cinnamon sticks and ginger. Bring to a boil and let it keep boiling on a high heat for 10 minutes. Remove the pan from the heat, then once it's cool, cover the pan and steep overnight.
2 litres water	
8–12 cloves	
4 bay leaves	
2 cinnamon sticks	
a thumb-sized piece of ginger, sliced	The next day, strain into a large bowl or jug. Add the sugar and bitters and stir until the sugar has dissolved.
400g caster sugar	You can now drink it as is over ice or dilute it with equal parts water. In Trinidad, we sometimes add a shot of rum. And while I always have this cold, my wife likes to drink it warm, like you would a mulled wine – it has those same Christmas flavours.
2 dashes of Angostura bitters	

RUM PUNCH

SERVES 4

My mum always made rum punch during Christmas in Nigeria and my older brother and sister would have some, but I could never have it because I was still a kid. So as soon as I was older, I couldn't wait to taste it. It did not disappoint!

90ml dark rum	Simply mix everything together and serve in a tall glass over ice.
60ml sugar syrup	
30ml freshly squeezed lime or lemon juice	
2 dashes of Angostura bitters	
a pinch of ground nutmeg	
ice, to serve	

INDEX

A
agege bread 57
akara (Nigerian bean fritters) 46
Angostura bitters 64
Auntie Angela's coconut bake 58

B
bake
    bake and hake 26
    fried bake 56
beans
    akara (Nigerian bean fritters) 46
    ewa agoyin 44
    moi moi (Nigerian steamed bean pudding) 49
    rice and peas 41
    spicy black-eyed beans 43
beef
    Nigerian red stew 12
    Nigerian suya (spicy beef skewers) 14
    stuffed peppers 16
bread
    agege bread 57
    Auntie Angela's coconut bake 58
    fried bake 56
brown stew chicken 10

C
carnival rice 40
Charmaine's chicken soup with dumplings 20
chicken
    brown stew chicken 10
    Charmaine's chicken soup with dumplings 20
    creamy coconut chicken curry 23
    JD's jerk chicken curry 18
    Nigerian pepper soup 24
    Socafro fried chicken 22
cinnamon puff-puff 60
coconut
    Auntie Angela's coconut bake 58
    creamy coconut chicken curry 23
    rice and peas 41
    Timea's coconut rice 42
    Trini curried prawns with coconut rice 28
creamy coconut chicken curry 23
curry
    creamy coconut chicken curry 23
    JD's jerk chicken curry 18
    Trini curried prawns with coconut rice 28

D
drinks
    rum punch 65
    sorrel 65
dumplings: Charmaine's chicken soup with dumplings 20

E
efo riro 32
eggs
    Indomie and eggs 35
    yam and eggs 34
egusi 33
ewa agoyin 44

F
fried bake 56
fried plantain 52
fritters: akara (Nigerian bean fritters) 46

G
gungo peas (pigeon peas): rice and peas 41

H
hake: bake and hake 26
hibiscus flowers: sorrel 65

I
ice cream: no-churn lemon-lime ice cream 62
Indomie and eggs 35

J
JD's jerk chicken curry 18
jollof rice 38

L

lemons: no-churn lemon-lime ice cream 62
limes
    no-churn lemon-lime ice cream 62
    rum punch 65

M

macaroni pie 54
mackerel: Socafro smoked mackerel 30
moi moi (Nigerian steamed bean pudding) 49

N

Nigerian pepper soup 24
Nigerian red stew 12
Nigerian suya (spicy beef skewers) 14
no-churn lemon-lime ice cream 62

O

obe ata (Nigerian red sauce) 8-9
    efo riro 32
    egusi 33
    ewa agoyin 44
    Nigerian red stew 12
    spicy black-eyed beans 43

P

peas: rice and peas 41
peppers
    jollof rice 38
    Nigerian pepper soup 24
    Nigerian red stew 12
    obe ata (Nigerian red sauce) 8-9
    stuffed peppers 16
plantain, fried 52
prawns
    Timea's coconut rice 42
    Trini curried prawns with coconut rice 28
puff-puff
    around the world 61
    cinnamon puff-puff 60

R

ramen noodles: Indomie and eggs 35
rice
    carnival rice 40
    jollof rice 38
    rice and peas 41
    Timea's coconut rice 42
    Trini curried prawns with coconut rice 28
rum punch 65

S

Socafro fried chicken 22
Socafro smoked mackerel 30
sorrel 65
soup
    Charmaine's chicken soup with dumplings 20
    Nigerian pepper soup 24
spicy black-eyed beans 43
spinach
    efo riro 32
    egusi 33
stew
    brown stew chicken 10
    efo riro 32
    Nigerian red stew 12
stuffed peppers 16

T

Timea's coconut rice 42
tomatoes
    efo riro 32
    egusi 33
    ewa agoyin 44
    Nigerian red stew 12
    obe ata (Nigerian red sauce) 8-9
Trini curried prawns with coconut rice 28

Y

yam
    yam and eggs 34
    yam three ways 50-51

Nine Bean Rows
23 Mountjoy Square
Dublin, D01 E0F8
Ireland
@9beanrowsbooks
ninebeanrowsbooks.com

Blasta Books is an imprint of Nine Bean Rows Books Ltd.
@blastabooks blastabooks.com

First published 2024

Text copyright © Alistair Jeje, 2024

Illustrations copyright © Nicky Hooper, 2024

ISBN: 978-1-7392105-6-4

Editor: Kristin Jensen

Series artist: Nicky Hooper
nickyhooper.com

Designer: Jane Matthews
janematthews.ie

Proofreader: Jocelyn Doyle

Printed by L&C Printing Group, Poland

The paper in this book is produced using pulp from managed forests.

All rights reserved.

No part of this publication may be copied, reproduced or transmitted in any form or by any means without written permission of the publishers.

A CIP catalogue record for this book is available from the British Library.

10 9 8 7 6 5 4 3 2 1

About the author

Alistair Jeje, affectionately known as JD, is the proud proprietor of Socafro Kitchen, a bustling street food venture in Waterford City offering an enticing fusion of Caribbean and Nigerian flavours. This culinary blend pays homage to his roots: his mother hails from Trinidad and his father from Nigeria. The name Socafro comes from JD's passion for two distinct music genres: the vibrant rhythms of Caribbean soca and the pulsating beats of Afro tunes.

JD was born in England but his formative years were spent in Lagos, where his mother and sister introduced him to the world of cooking. JD believes that your true calling is what you can do effortlessly, and for him, cooking is just that. JD's larger-than-life charisma is undeniably magnetic, and his radiant smile and treasured recipes lift up everyone who meets him and eats his food.

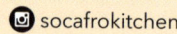 socafrokitchen